Nort

CW00497299

One Man in a Pocket

Robert Wingfield

50% of royalties from sales of this book will be donated to
Kyrenia Animal Rescue
http://www.kartrnc.org/index.html

NORTH CYPRUS

THE POCKET GUIDE

First Edition

CONTENTS

1.   WHY YOU MIGHT NEED THIS BOOK

You may have already seen my full version of a guided tour around North Cyprus in the *One Man in a Bus* series, but readers have been asking for something focusing on places to visit and detailing concise points, to carry around with them. So here it is, a short guidebook to North Cyprus; the font is necessarily small in paperback because there is so much information I need to share, that if it was any bigger, the guide would be the size of a brick! With this in your pocket (and it will fit – I've tried it), you can visit and appreciate many of the locations, and learn a bit of the history and the legends while you travel. Some places and names are highlighted if you want to do further background research, and there is a list of websites at the end, to get you started.

North Cyprus is about the size of Cornwall in the UK, but you will probably need your own transport (or an accommodating taxi driver) to get around most effectively. For a base location, **Kyrenia** is as good as any, and the order of the sites to visit is loosely based on this assumption.

There are many **hotels** of varying, but reasonable, prices. You may prefer the smaller, family-run establishments because you will get to know the people as well as the place, and they can give you extra hints and tips to further improve your enjoyment.

For hotels, look here first: https://www.tripadvisor.co.uk/Hotels-g190378-Kyrenia_Kyrenia_District-Hotels.html

Robert Wingfield March 2016

1

2.   THE MAP

In the following map, the stars are approximations of the locations detailed, numbers referring to chapters.

Our exploration is confined to the north of the white line roughly indicating the border. For more accurate details, you should get one of the excellent touring maps available from tourist offices — contact particulars at time of publishing are given in the appendix.

The east-west scale of the map is correct, but north-south has been expanded slightly to fit the page and give you more room to scribble notes (and abuse).

After the map, we launch straight into the sites and sights, so please enjoy your holiday, starting here.

Relief map modified from Wikipedia -

https://en.wikipedia.org/wiki/File:Cyprus_topo.png

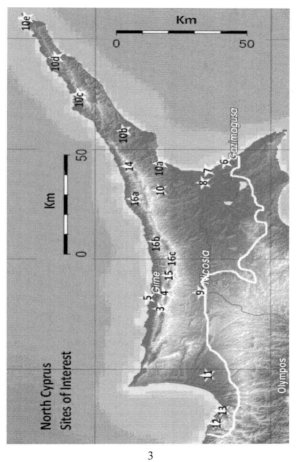

North Cyprus
Sites of Interest

3. ST HILARION CASTLE

St Hilarion Castle is not far from Kyrenia. It is the one on the peak that you can see from many places in the town, but is nearly ¾ of a kilometre above hotel level. Using your hired car (or a local taxi) you can find it by leaving the main Nicosia road in the mountains, turning right up a series of hairpins towards the summit. Once on this challenging ascent, you will pass a military base, one of many dotting open areas of the country. Don't take any pictures of the soldiers; they have guns and may be terrible shots. In North Cyprus, teenagers do 15 months national service to give them backbone and teach them how to make bullet holes.

Past the base is a flat bit of mountain where knights of old used to joust. It is now being used as a firing range. From your vantage point, they will look so close to the targets that they might as well be on a 'throwing' range. There are warning signs not to enter this area; a wise statement, there must be any number of stray bullets flying across the countryside. Luckily there is a wire fence with a warning sign on it between you and them.

Below the summit, there is a car park and you are well advised to get out here and walk the rest of the way. The space right by the gate itself is normally wedged with coaches, balancing on a 20% incline.

The castle is built on top of a mountain, and was originally created as a watchtower for early warning against Arab raids, later being converted to a more extensive castle by the Crusaders. Beware uneven surfaces. Stout walking footgear is recommended. Don't forget that there have been 300 years of Lusignan boots wearing the steps and walkways down.

St Hilarion's (291-371) day is October 21st. He was widely travelled and is reputed to have settled on Cyprus in the latter years of his life. However, this is possibly not the same man as a later St Hilarion, after whom the place is named. The **Byzantine** rulers built a chapel to him in the castle during the 9th Century. Surprisingly it is still largely intact, but this is because it has been altered and repaired over time. See if you can spot the modifications.

In 1191, it was captured from the beleaguered Byzantine Empire by **Guy de Lusignan**, acting on the orders of **Richard 1st of England** who was leading the **Third Crusade**. Richard needed finance to bash Saracens, so he sold the Island to the **Knights Templar**, who paid him in an early form of travellers' cheques, giving them the dubious distinction of being the first real 'bankers' in history. The Templars tried to raise the cash from the Islanders, who very soon got annoyed and refused to cover Richard's subsequent demands for solid silver (an early banking crisis – nothing changes). After a sally from St Hilarion where the Templars murdered everyone they met (unlike real bankers, thank goodness), they decided to leave, and sold the country to Guy, who became the first of the **Lusignan rulers in 1192**.

The castle was strengthened over the years and was fully organised for defence by 1228. The last action it saw was in 1232 when the **Lombards** overran the Island, and would have eventually starved out the defenders if a relief force hadn't arrived from campaigns in Syria.

After this there were 140 years of calm. The castle became a summer residence and royal palace to escape from the heat of the lowlands, and an occasional retreat from arbitrary invaders.

When the **Venetians** took the country over in 1489, they 'slighted' the castle (destroyed the fortifications) to prevent it being used tactically in future. The place was eventually abandoned, because potential attacks would be coming by sea, not air, and it made more sense to live by the shoreline where they could protect the harbours.

With some restoration work to repair further damage over the years, it is in this condition today.

Beware, the **Nanny State** doesn't apply here, and '**Health and Safety**' relates to some other country. In consequence you can wander most places and actually enjoy the castle as it should be. There are safety rails and warning signs though, which give some indication of where you might plummet to your death, so it is essential that you stay the correct side of these.

Going up the mountain, you start with the lower section where peasants and soldiers lived, and then move on up to see the actual **Church of St Hilarion**. Have a look into the **Bellavista Hall** where the mediaeval ladies of Guy de Lusignan, after toiling upwards without the aid of diesel engine, were too tired to climb back down, and would gather to watch the jousting on the firing range a mile or so away. There are another 300 steps to the **Royal Apartments**.

Investigate the ruins there and notice the **Queen's Window**, facing west to pick up the prevailing wind and keep the concubines cool during the long hot months of mediaeval summer.

Water was collected off the roofs of the buildings in **cisterns**, big lead-lined holes excavated in the limestone, thus removing the need to get a dodgy plumber in. So good are these, that some of the cisterns still contain (stagnant) water. Wonder about the health of the people who would have had to drink it. They probably didn't really live long enough to suffer the effects of lead poisoning, but the water can't have tasted all that wholesome, (although the poison would keep out other bugs). They probably had a 'buttery', and made beer - not butter - for the inhabitants to drink instead. There are waxwork displays of what some of the inhabitants might have looked like, and they do look a little intoxicated.

Before you leave, you really must try the **lemonade** at the café by the entrance (you may have already done this on the way in of course). It is very lemony and perhaps a bit sweet for some people, but will be cooling and most welcome after the scaling of the castle in the warmth of the day.

4. BELLAPAIS ABBEY

In the UK, most of our religious institutions were knocked down when **Henry VIII** decided that he fancied a charming young English thing over the older foreign lady he had been saddled with. It will be no surprise therefore to find **Bellapais Abbey** in a similar condition. This has an ancient church attached to it, and was founded as a place of pilgrimage and retreat by exiled clergy who still thought they should be living in **Jerusalem**. They couldn't of course, because they had been kicked out by Selahaddin Eyyubi ('**Saladin**', because one name is never enough) in 1187. Cyprus has a history of housing clergy and **'kings' of Jerusalem** who could never win enough wars to capture the place back. The word 'titular' comes to mind, but this may be only for the comedy value.

The abbey was built between 1198 and 1205 by **Augustinian** monks and was originally called 'The Abbey of Saint Mary of the Mountain'. The Augustinians were soon followed by the **White Canons or Norbertines**, following **Saint Norbert** (feast day June 6th), who called it '**The White Abbey**' to save time. The Venetians came and in true tradition changed the name again, this time to **De la Paix**, ('Of Peace') and then because it had only had three names so far, which was well below average for any place in Cyprus, it eventually became **Bellapais** (Abbaye de la Belle Paix), giving its name to the attached village, which is also well worth a look.

When the **Ottomans took over in 1571**, in a fit of generosity they allowed it to be re-dedicated to the **Greek Orthodox** church, who blocked up the nave so that the peasants couldn't see what was going on behind, and promptly let the rest of the place fall apart.

As is usual with a beautiful and priceless building, the peasantry soon started filching the stones to build their hovels, and over the years, 'abandoned' became 'ruined' and 'plundered'.

The refectory, a large dinner hall, still survives and was later used as a store room. Built with sturdy buttresses on the edge of the cliff, it has stood the test of time, through earthquake and firestorm.

When the **British** arrived in **1878**, fresh from supporting the **Ottomans** in their latest spat with **Russia**, they cemented the floor up and turned the refectory into a field hospital. What sort of hospital it was, we can only guess, as you can see where they used the end wall for target practice.

The refectory and the vault on the garden side are used to stage concerts to raise money for local causes and also for the **TRNC's Music Festival** (21st May for four weeks). The acoustics are reported to be gorgeous. Weddings are conducted in the **Kybele Restaurant** adjacent to the Abbey and then photos in the grounds afterwards.

Everywhere in the abbey there are bits of stone nicked from **Salamis**, including a **sarcophagus** they used for water to wash their hands, and Roman columns incorporated to hold up various roofs. When you visit Salamis, be surprised when you find there is lots still left to see, despite all this plunder.

Other points of note are **Gothic stone carvings** still intact, as well as **masons' marks** on some of the higher up stonework.

In the Abbey grounds, you will see an ancient tree that originally had both limes and lemons grafted on to the same stem, presumably to see if it would work. It did for a few years, but the limes have reclaimed their rights now and it is just a tree again. Don't pick the fruit, otherwise there will be nothing on it for anyone else to see.

There is another tree here, called '**The Tree of Idleness'**, under which the elders of the village gather during the day to drink coffee and talk politics. This permitted them to avoid any work and to allow their women to toil, keeping house, field and home together. There are many similar places - most villages have one.

Writer **Laurence Durrell** had a three year stopover in Bellapais. He would have stayed longer but the **partisans** were determined to throw the British out, and made life too dangerous to stay. These terrorists did eventually succeed, and in 1960 the British left, sobbing and saying they were only doing their best really. This gave the new government free rein to kill their own people in the name of 'nationalism' without anyone trying to stop them - you may have guessed by now that the Greeks and Turks are not best chums (the animosity goes back a very long way). Laurence wrote '**Bitter Lemons**' (1957), which summed up the situation quite nicely and might interest readers who want to find out what it was like then. He is not to be confused with his brother, Gerald, who was also there, but was more interested in animals than politics.

5. KYRENIA

Kyrenia harbour predates the Romans, being in all likelihood one of the thirteen (ten or twelve - sources don't seem to be able to agree) city kingdoms founded around 500 BC, (see the General Information section) and now is surrounded by cafés, where once there were warehouses storing **carob beans**, a staple diet of peasants and livestock alike. Carob is also used for making chocolate and syrup, which are local favourites and make a good cake.

There are a few expensive yachts in the harbour but not as many as in the heyday of the elite before the troubles and economic meltdown of the last decades. It is everyone's hope that things will improve.

The Castle dates back to the 7th Century, Byzantine in foundation, built to protect the harbour and town from **Arab raids**. The central buildings are all gone, but there is a pile of loose masonry left over (some of it suspiciously Romanesque) so if you did decide to rebuild, you would have something to start with.

After the invention of gunpowder, the Lusignan walls had new Venetian walls built in front of them, and the space in-between filled with rubble to create a sponge effect, hopefully absorbing the impact of cannon-balls. All that work was never needed; the Venetians gave up the castle without a fight when invading Ottomans approached in 1570, sporting the heads of Venetian leaders from Nicosia on sticks.

Once the British arrived, they dug out the rubble between the two sets of walls and discovered the small **Byzantine Church of St George**, now gently repaired. Quarters for ancient notables were converted into cells for political activists, and the castle became a military headquarters and secure prison for Turkish prisoners during the First World War, and possibly the **EOKA** (Ethniki Organosis Kyprion Agoniston), The National Organization of Cypriot Fighters determined to evict the British during the troubles of 1955-1959.

It was only fully opened to the public in 1974.

Things to see include dark passages down to the **gun emplacements** put in by the Venetians and giving a field of fire along the moat in various directions, and the **dungeon** with what are translated as 'animations', but are in fact waxworks, including one poor soul in a state of undress on a torture wheel, and a lady down an oubliette.

There is a good display of the **Akdeniz Village Tomb**, the Neolithic settlement at **Vrysi**, and the **Kirni Bronze Age tomb**. **The Shipwreck museum** features displays and the remains of an actual merchant ship sunk during the **4th Century BC**. Possibly the oldest example in the world.

In the centre of the courtyard is a set of steps leading down to one of the **original cisterns**, which appears to have some of the original water still in it. As you can imagine, it whiffs a bit, and there are extractors to help you breathe, if you can find the right switch to operate.

A walk around the **outside of the castle** in the evening is to be recommended. After dark, it's a bit gloomy on the far side, but you never feel threatened, and crime is almost unheard of.

In the rest of the town, the **Ancient Roman Rock Tombs**, are not officially open to the public, but the gates may have been forced so you can investigate if you are brave enough. Take a torch.

The Icon Museum is being refurbished at the moment, so if they haven't finished, visit **St Mamas in Güzelyurt** instead if you are keen on seeing Byzantine art.

Do try to visit the **Kyrenia Animal Rescue** shop and support this charity who look after most of the strays you will meet. You will find it east on the Catalkoy Road. The rescue centre itself is in the **Beşparmak** mountains, near **Arapkoy** about 20Km south-east of Kyrenia.

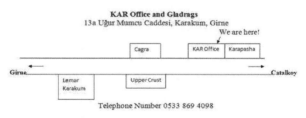

KAR Office and Gladrags
13a Uğur Mumcu Caddesi, Karakum, Girne

Telephone Number 0533 869 4098

Open: Monday to Sunday 9.00am - 1.00pm

https://www.facebook.com/KyreniaAnimalRescuekar/info

6.   FAMAGUSTA

For your trip to Famagusta, from Kyrenia, there is a long drive over the hills called the '**Five Finger Mountains**', sometimes referred to as '**Beşparmak**' and others '**Pendadactylos**'. One of these crags looks like a clenched fist. The legend is that two men were fighting over a girl. The bad one pushed the good one into a marsh. As the poor fellow sank, he raised his sword in a final effort and killed the bad man, thus saving the lovely lady from a life of unpleasantness. Sadly though, the good man couldn't stop himself sinking, and the last that was seen of him was his raised hand. The marsh dried out and the land sank and his fist can still be seen. The story doesn't say what happened to the girl, but one wonders if it involved carob and slaving in the fields.

There are only five passes through the mountains, and this one is within sight of the Animal Rescue sanctuary.

On the way down the other side, you pass limestone quarries and military training grounds for the first few miles, and can see Nicosia in the far distance across the plain.

There are many partially built houses and blocks on the **central plain**. These were abandoned owing to austerity, tax reasons or forced migration. Much of the building work relates to 2004, when there was a huge building boom due to the proposed **Annan Plan** and the assumption that there would be a settlement between the two sides. It never happened and unfortunately a lot of new buildings were neglected.

14

You will see that each village has its own mosque. These days there are more Turkish settlers, bringing the stricter culture of Islam with them, but the Cypriot locals are not generally bothered and still do their own thing. The mosques are funded from Turkey.

Going east on the main road, you eventually reach **Famagusta**, which is also known as 'Mağusa' and occasionally 'Gazimagusta'. Famagusta is known to the Greeks as Ammohostos, poignantly meaning 'Buried in the sand'.

To the south of the city you might be able to see the tower blocks of the **Ghost Town**, or **Varosha**. Nobody is allowed in to that area, and it is guarded by Turkish troops. It is in such a sad state of repair, damaged by the gunfire of the **1974 Turkish invasion**, that it would need to be levelled first and a new start made before resettling. It is said that the car showrooms still have 1974 models in the windows, if you are looking for that never ending restoration project, but there is a good chance someone has beaten you to it. Varosha is a bone of contention between the Turkish and Greek Cypriots. This is a great shame as it has one of the best beaches in the country.

Enter the central walled town across a narrow bridge through the **Land Gate**. You can get a car through if you fancy your chances inside and may even be able to find somewhere to park.

The following sights are listed in no particular order.

The Land Gate

Built in 1544 and also known as the Half-moon Bastion. On the town side are underground chambers originally used as dungeons.

Sinan Pasha Mosque

The **Sinan Pasha Mosque** was originally the Lusignan church of St Peter and St Paul, and known as the '**Wheat Mosque**' owing to it being used for storage after the Ottomans arrived. This may still be undergoing renovations, but outside is the **Tomb of Yirmisekiz Mehmed Çelebi**. He was the first Ottoman ambassador to Europe (France) in 1720 and his appreciation of the local broadsheets triggered the arrival of the **printing press** in Istanbul .

The Venetian Palace

The ruins of the **Venetian palace (1550)** seem to be mostly a carpark. The palace took a battering during the Ottoman invasion, and there is a wonderful assortment of cannon-balls collected as part of that. Some are under wire netting because people were helping themselves - now you know what is in all those huge bags taken on the plane as 'hand luggage'. The door to the palace opened on to the largest central square in Europe at the time. There is still a three-arched entrance on **Namik Kemal Square**, constructed from Roman columns plundered from Salamis (of course).

The city could have held out indefinitely against the Ottomans, but they were abandoned by Venice and after 11 months, supplies ran out and surrender was the only option. The defenders were allowed to leave the city peacefully, but when the Ottomans learned that some Muslim prisoners had been killed during the siege, they had **Bragadin**, the Venetian commander, flayed alive and sent his skin off to Constantinople (as you do).

The Turkish Bath - Cafér Pasha Hamam (1601)

In the north-west corner of Namik Kemal Square is the fountain and **Turkish Bath** from 1601-1605. The bath is now a restaurant so you can eat there and try to imagine what it was like. There is another example in Nicosia, which can be seen as it used to be.

The Dungeon of the Poet Namik Kemal

This is also in the courtyard of the Venetian Palace, and the poet was kept here for over three years for denouncing the Ottoman government in his play, **Vatan Yahut Silistre**.

Lala Mustafa Pasha Mosque

Across the square is the main **Cathedral of St Nicholas**, which is now the **Lala Mustafa Pasha Mosque**, stripped of all its Lusignan finery apart from the Gothic tracery of the windows. The **Mihrab** (wall niche facing **Mecca**) is pointing not quite at Mecca because of the building being oriented on Christian lines. There are some small carved statues over the doorway which may have been originally plastered over, but are perfectly preserved without weather damage. If you can get into the women's refuge, inside is the tomb slab of a bishop from Lusignan times. The other tomb slabs are still under the carpet, but were turned face down by the Ottomans because they were in a hurry to convert it.

This was the building in which the original **Kings of Cyprus** were crowned a second time as '**Kings of Jerusalem**', despite not being allowed over there by the Muslim occupiers.

Outside the main entrance is one of the **oldest trees** in the country, over 700 years and a species of tropical fig - **Ficus Sycomorus**.

It was in this courtyard that a massacre occurred during the coronation of **James II** (also called 'James the Bastard') in 1471. He was the **last King of Cyprus** (and Jerusalem - yes, the Lusignans still thought they owned it, despite not being over there for 300 years). There was a small altercation outside when the king arrived, presumably the peasants calling him by his nickname, and this quickly escalated when the king's faction decided to discuss politics with the other, and slaughtered them all. This made him not a popular king.

James did survive another three years, where he started to forge ties with Venice, who were expanding their influence in the eastern Mediterranean, and then both he and his baby son unexpected died within a few weeks of each other, leaving his wife **Caterina Cornaro** (then 19 and presumably an ambitious girl) to rule. She held it together for another five years before surrendering the country to the Venetians on **26th February 1489**, ironically in the same cathedral.

After you have seen the Mosque (in socked feet), go around the corner for a coffee break in a charming café near the Sea Gate that also does the best selection of cakes in town.

The Sea Gate

Built in **Italian Renaissance style in 1496** it features an Ottoman wooden door on the land side and a Venetian portcullis on the sea side. Above the gate is the winged Lion of St Mark, carved in marble probably recovered from Salamis.

Othello Castle

The Castle, also called Κάστρο της Οθέλλου in Greek and **Othello Kulesi** in Turkish was named by the British occupiers in the 19th Century because they had worked out that Shakespeare had been visiting in 1589 when he nicked the idea for the play of the same name from an earlier story. The name seems to have stuck.

The original **14th Century Lusignan** fort was modified by the Venetians, removing the upper levels, rounding the towers and thickening the walls. It is not as feature-rich as the Crusader castles, being purely a military defensive structure. It is well worth a visit though, to see how the alterations were applied, and for the excellent views of the City. At this stage you cannot get into the sections formally occupied by the cannons (you can see what they are like by visiting Kyrenia Castle), but you can get to the top of the north-east tower for sightseeing. The holes to let cannon smoke out are covered by fragile plastic.

All that remains down below seem to be the lower levels of the stonework, and a load of interesting tunnels which are currently blocked by small barriers.

It has been open to the public since only July 2015 after renovations by Spanish contractors, which may still be ongoing.

Churches of the Knights Templar and Hospitallers.

Both are dedicated to St John. The larger belonged to the Templars (aka the Chapel of St Antonio) but when they were dissolved in 1312 by **Pope Clement V**, the Hospitallers (Knights of St John) took it over, and decided to build their own church next door. These have recently been restored and there are frescoes to be viewed.

The Church of St Francis of Assisi (13th 14th C)

Very ruined but there are buttresses still to be seen. There was a monastery attached, but this has completely disappeared.

St George of the Latins (13th C)

Well ruined but with elegant columns to support the roof and a few carvings you can have fun trying to identify.

St George of the Greeks (14th C)

A mixture of Gothic and Orthodox styles with arched niches and vague traces of frescoes of a 15th C Italianate style. There are still

Ottoman cannonballs embedded in the walls. Resist the temptation to use your penknife to get them out again.

The Nestorian Church of St George Xorinos

Currently used as a cultural centre for the Eastern Mediterranean University, it also hosts Sunday services for the Anglican community. It has a rose window above the entrance and a few frescoes remain inside in good condition.

The Museum and Tomb of Canbulat

Canbulat was the leader of the Ottoman attack on the city, and the legend is that he had his head cut off and carried it under his arm for the three days of the final attack. Oddly, this gave the invading forces the motivation to continue and take the castle. As a place of pilgrimage for Turks, his tomb ranks second in Cyprus to the shrine of **Hala Sultan Tekke at Larnaca**.

There was allegedly a fig tree by his tomb, that would promote fertility in any woman who ate the fruit, so watch out girls!

Montinengo Bastion

Leaving the city towards Salamis, note the massive **Montinengo Bastion**, which was thought to be, and actually probably was, impregnable, at least to the Ottomans, who decided to lob their collection of hardware over the top. The breach in the nearby walls was made by the British to get larger vehicles inside the city.

7. SALAMIS

The City of Enkomi (Tuzla)

Originally on a navigable river, Enkomi was a centre for the processing of copper ore. There was an earthquake in 1200BC, and another in 1075BC, after which the river silted up and the townsfolk lost heart and ships and moved nearer the coast to found Salamis. There are still ruins to be seen at this site.

Salamis

Between 800 and 400 BC, Salamis controlled lands as far as the Troodos mountains, but after the death of **Alexander the Great** (Alexander III of Macedon - 356-323 BC), was mostly ruled by Egypt up to the Roman annexation in 58 BC.

Roman and then Byzantine (Eastern Roman Empire based in Constantinople) rule extended until 1191, but after 648, the main port was moved to Famagusta. Plundering by the Venetians later removed many columns and artefacts, but shifting sands have protected the city from further looting; 90% of the site is still covered, but it is not known when further archaeological excavations will take place. It all depends on the long-term stability of the country, but with luck that won't be long and we will be able to properly enjoy the full extent of a city which could rival Pompeii in its splendour.

The Theatre at Salamis

The building has been partially reconstructed but is still a magnificent 20 tiers high, which can hold up to 5000 spectators. Originally it was 50 tiers, with a maximum capacity of 15,000. From this, if we assume that the richer half of the population would visit, that gives an estimate of up to 30,000 souls at the time it was built.

Beware of sand-fly bites here. If you linger, sit higher up and enjoy the views and the atmosphere.

Gymnasium and baths

In this excavated complex, there is a semi-circular 40-seater toilet, and you might see lizards the size of squirrels, totally harmless of course, but don't try to catch one. Marvel at how the Roman plumbing worked: the water would be continually running as it overflowed from the bathing pools, through the toilet and thence out to sea.

Notable amongst the remains is a superb example of a hypocaust in the caldarium, and a fresco and two mosaics in archways.

There are many headless statues surrounding the north pool. One theory is that the bodies were made in advance and the heads were changed as notables went in and out of favour. Where are the heads now? Nobody knows, but you might suspect they were in the hand luggage of the people who block the aisles when getting on the plane.

The Agora

This was originally the market place and had covered walkways around two sides, to protect shops and shoppers from the elements. There is still one column the Venetians didn't take.

The Cistern

Water was brought 50Km from a spring in **Kythrea (Değirmenlik)** near the **Herbarium**, via an aqueduct, three arches of which can still be seen a few miles outside Salamis. The largest cistern was supported by 36 square pillars.

The Campanopetra Basilica

A 4th Century structure, which has a well, a lectern, remains of a bath and some more mosaics .

The Villa

To the south of the theatre is remains of an influential person's city house.

St Epiphanios Basilica

Beyond the villa, the basilica was the largest in Cyprus when it was built in 400AD. The eponymous bishop's tomb can still be seen, encased in marble in the southern apse.

The Temple of Zeus

Sadly, little remains of this, but there were inscriptions discovered, honouring Livia, the consort of Emperor Augustus.

The Cellarka Necropolis

About 350 metres away and towards the village of Tuzla is the necropolis. There are over 100 tombs carved into a strip of hard limestone, and was used for the more common townsfolk up until about 400BC, when they ran out of space.

St Catherine's Prison

Officially 'Tomb 50' of the necropolis complex, but well worth a visit.

St Catherine, born around 287AD, was the daughter of **King Constant of Cyprus**. Maxentius, the ruler of Alexandria and son of the emperor **Diocletian**, tried to get her to change her faith, without success, torturing her and throwing her into prison. He asked, it is said, fifty philosophers and orators to convince Catherine to return to the Roman religions. She countered their arguments to such an extent that she converted them to Christianity as well. For their new beliefs, they were burned at the stake.

Maxentius finally ordered that Catherine should be severely beaten and tied to a rolling spiked wheel (the origin of the firework, Catherine Wheel?) Although she survived this torture, she was beheaded in 307 and was later canonised for her beliefs.

After all that excitement, try the local restaurant for lunch. The food and the views are superb.

8.   ST BARNABAS

A short drive from Salamis is the monastery of the saint who was the companion of St Paul until they went their separate ways. St Paul did the better of the two, being executed publicly in Rome, but despite all his best efforts, including writing a gospel of his own, Barnabas is largely forgotten. He was finally murdered by a group of 'Syrians' at Salamis in 75AD. Before they got to him however, he did manage to convert the governor of **Paphos**, **Sergius Paulus**, who became the first ever Christian ruler in 46 AD (well before Constantine the Great, 306-337 AD).

Barnabas' body was secretly buried under a carob tree, much to the annoyance of the pursuing Jews, who wanted to throw him in the sea instead. Barnabas became the patron saint of Cyprus.

The church is not massive, and although it was started 2000 years ago, has been successively rebuilt by each of the major occupiers. There are **Corinthian capitals** poking out through the plaster, reminding us again to be grateful that there is still anything left at Salamis. There are many icons here; these are not the funny little pictures on your fondleslab screen, but actually stylised paintings of the saints and other holy personages. Some are better than others, and several were completed by the last guardians of the monastery, the three brothers **Charitan, Stephanos and Barnabas**, who stayed with it until 'retiring' in 1976. From 1991, restoration work has been ongoing.

There is a good museum, containing examples of ancient local pottery and amphorae, and a gift shop containing examples of modern local scarves at imaginative prices (in Euros). See if you can spot a superb example of recycling, where a toy chariot has been made out of a broken pot by some resourceful ancient parent.

On the way down the hill from the monastery to see the mausoleum, beware as you pass an unfenced excavation believed to be part of the Salamis necropolis (don't fall down the holes). Note the way the tombs are packed together. As space ran out, the dead were buried in a warren resembling an inverted Jenga tower. The archaeologists must have had some fun removing the bodies without the whole place collapsing, and them losing the game.

The tomb of Saint Barnabas himself is in a little mausoleum past the cemetery and down a few steps on the left of the door to a recess containing a shrouded coffin. It is a humble but humbling place.

9. NICOSIA

Nicosia is also called **Lefkoşa** by the Turkish Cypriots and Λευκωσία by the Greeks. This is now the only capital city in the world still split between two countries. The following are details of what to see in the North City, but feel free to cross the border at the **Ledra Palace Border Crossing** – on foot or bicycle only. You will need your passport.

Enter by the Kyrenia gate, which actually has four names to show how important it was. The others are: Girne Kapısı, Πύλη της Κερύνειας and Porta del Proveditore ('Proveditore' is the Venetian for 'military governor').

As one might expect, the original gate is standing isolated, separated from the walls either side, another thoroughfare modified by the British. Looking at the size of the actual gate opening, it is just as well really. Not only would you have a job to squeeze a camel through the original entrance, but you would also cause havoc amongst the displays in the Tourist Office inside.

Either side of the gateway you can see the massive town walls, built by the Venetians as a formidable line of defences, featuring impregnable bastions, and bristling with gun ports. They knew three years in advance that the Ottomans were on their way, and would have had the fortifications completed in plenty of time had the leaders not been arguing amongst themselves for most of it. Nothing changes does it?

The Ottomans duly popped over and laid siege. After a few weeks, they found out where the new ramparts had only been mocked up, and strolled into town on 9th September 1570. The invaders slaughtered 20,000, mostly male, citizens, and the arguing generals paid the price in the swift removal of their heads for presentation to the garrison of Kyrenia, which encouraged those worthies to open their own gates without a fight.

Museum of the Whirling Dervishes

A few metres inside the walls from the Kyrenia Gate, there is an opening on the left – try not to miss it, because this is the museum.

The **Dervishes** were a group of peace-loving Sufi monks who achieved enlightenment by spinning in floaty dresses and wearing fearsome moustaches. There are 16 tombs of departed **Mevlevihane** sheiks here, still with their hats on. Their overall message, as with all religions, is one of peace, but this one was special.

The Mevlevi order (of Sufism) was founded by the poet **Mevlana Celaleddin Rumi**, born in Afghanistan in 1207. When he was very young, his parents emigrated to Anatolia and settled in Konya, where he studied history, theology and the philosophy of law and devised his own variation of Islam. Mevlana was a Muslim, but not orthodox; his doctrine advocated unlimited tolerance, positive reasoning, goodness, charity and awareness through love. **To him all beliefs were valid, not only his own.**

The mystical philosophy that he expressed in his poetry and bequeathed to the Mevlevi order spread east to India, and then across the entire Islamic world. His teachings emphasised the individual soul's separation from God during earthly existence, and the power of Divine Love to draw it back upon death.

The (now) saint stressed music and dance as an expression of this mutual love and yearning, and the Mevlevi order became famous for its whirling ceremony. In Cyprus, the **Lefkoşa Mevlevihane** (where you now are) was the centre of the Sufi tradition.

The Tekkes (Dervish Lodges) in the Turkish republic were closed in 1925, and the Mevlevi order moved to Aleppo in Syria; goodness knows where they are based now, but evidence of them can be seen in Istanbul and Texas as well as locally. Although the majority of Turkish Cypriots were in favour of the closure, the British colonial administration on the island allowed the tradition to continue. In 1956, the Tekke was converted into a hostel for Turkish children under care. It closed in 1961, was mostly demolished for a shopping centre in 1970, and then the remains finally opened as a museum in 2002.

There are Dervish performances at times and cost in various locations, and well worth seeing.

Rumi's poetry is still studied and widespread in many cultures.

Dr Fazıl Küçük Museum

Fazil was the founder of the newspaper, Halkin Sesi (The Voice of the People), and campaigned against the British as a supporter of independence. Ironically, despite hating the occupiers, he died in 1984 in a London hospital.

The Samanbahçe Quarter

Near the Venetian Column, this was an attempt at social housing to revive the traditional Turkish neighbourhood. It is worth a walk through, but is reported as being in need of a bit of TLC.

The Venetian Column

Standing in **Ataturk Square**, which is known locally as the **Sarayönü** and was called **Konak Square** during the British presence, the Column is yet another plundered artefact from Salamis, again by the Venetians, from 1489. It is made of granite and they originally topped it with a small statue of the Lion of St Mark. It was toppled by the Ottomans and lay forgotten for centuries until the British re-erected it in 1915. They could not find the original statue, which is probably now in some private collection, so instead a shiny bronze orb was put on top.

Also off the Square are the **British Colonial Law Courts**.

The centre of the city is run down, most of the bigger shops being out in the suburbs, and is now inhabited by poor immigrants from the mainland.

The Arab Ahmet Mosque and Quarter

Dating from the early 16thC, this mosque has a dome 6m in diameter and is one of only two in the country with the 'dome on square' format. There is a fountain and a small graveyard, one of the tombs housing **Mehmed Kâmil Pasha**, who was four times Grand Vizier of the Ottoman Empire.

Dervish Pasha Mansion

This is a museum built in the Ottoman style, originally a private house, but refurbished and opened in 1988 to display various artefacts used by the local people. The architecture is worth seeing, as well as the inner courtyard, and will take you back 200 years in your mind. Coffee is sometimes available, and worth it for the experience.

The Armenian Church and Monastery

Surrounded by a boundary wall, there are three Armenian school buildings, the premises of the Armenian Prelacy (church leaders), an important historical mansion, and several courtyards.

The Church contains significant architectural and decorative elements from the original 14thC construction, including frescoes, carved bosses and capitals, and tracery and metal elements originally holding stained-glass.

The Büyük Hamam

The **Great Turkish Bath** was built on the ruins of a 14thC Lusignan church and the rooms are now 2-3 metres below ground level owing to the build-up of the surrounding roads. There is a changing room and warm and cold sections. Light comes in from holes in the bell-shaped cupola.

The Kumarcilar (Gamblers') Khan

Built on the ruins of an earlier structure (perhaps a monastery) in the early 1700s, this became an inn, similar in use to the Great Khan. It was known as The **Gambers' Khan**, and then later **The Travelling Minstrels Khan**, accommodating the musicians for many ceremonies that took place in the nearby square..

Ayia Sophia

Ayia Sophia means 'Holy Wisdom' and not necessarily after a saint called Sophia, despite the cathedral also being called St Sophia. It is now a mosque of course. In Turkish it is called 'Selimiye Camii', and Greek, Σελιμιγιέ Τζαμί). Entry is free.

Here you must remove your shoes, knees and shoulders from sight, and pad about on the thick but uneven carpet covering the inverted tombstones of past Christian monks - when the conversion took place, on 15th September 1571, less than a week after the massacre of all the men in town, there was not enough black-stone to be had to replace the floor, so the tomb slabs were simply turned face down to hide the Christian inscriptions. The same of course happened in Famagusta a year later.

The original stained glass has been replaced with simple but pleasing light diffusers, and all the original trappings have been removed.

The **Mihrab** here does face **Mecca**, unlike the mosque in Famagusta, and the lines on the relatively new carpet likewise. There are the other features, such as the place where the women can pray, and the **Mimbar** (pulpit) from where sermons and speeches are given.

Note the massive stone pillars, built to withstand earthquakes, and the beautiful vaulted roof, and then leave and wander around the quaint little streets nearby for photo opportunities.

The Bedesten

Closely beside Aiya Sophia, is the **Bedesten**, the original **Church of St Nicholas**, now largely used for Dervish performances, and jealously guarded by fearsome bearded chaps, wanting entrance fees in Euros, not Lira.

It was originally a Byzantine basilica from the 6th Century. A new church was built on the remains by the followers of **Thomas à Becket** in the late 12th, and then yet another on top of that by the Lusignans in the 14th.

The Ottomans converted it to a bedesten (covered textile market), and then used it progressively for storing food, flour and wheat. Between 2004-9, it was renovated and is now used as a cultural centre. There are still ruins attached to the main building.

The Bandabulya

This is a covered market in current use, has many stalls and shops selling souvenirs and carpets, and the best Turkish Delight in the country. Don't forget to haggle over prices as the shopkeepers feel let down if they are able to sell their wares for what they are asking.

The Great Khan

Again nearby, this wonderful building is acknowledged as one of the island's most important Ottoman works of architecture. Built between 1572 and 1579, the Great Khan is a lovely square structure in limestone, and its 68 rooms were originally used as shops below and hotel accommodation above. It was also known as a Caravanserai (roadside inn) or Souk (open air market place), as it served both purposes. In ancient times they bolted the doors at night to protect the travellers and their stock. Allegedly the warmest place to sleep was with the animals, but don't try this at home if you keep tigers. There are examples of this type of building still used as hotels in many other countries, including Morocco. The rooms may be a bit small and claustrophobic, but it is an experience all the same.

Today it has a number of cafés and many shops selling a better quality of gifts than some others, at a better quality of price. Stop for a drink in one of the outside cafes while you explore.

The Ledra Palace Border Crossing

This is for foot travellers only and opened on April 3rd 2008. You will get through without any difficulty, but make sure you have your passport.

The Lapidary Museum

A museum of stone fragments doesn't sound too interesting, but do stop for a visit. There are coats of arms, marble, columns and sarcophagi taken from the demolition of ancient buildings amongst other exhibits. It is situated a few hundred metres from the Selimiye Mosque (St. Sophia) and the building is believed to have originally been a 15thC Venetian house.

The Haydarpaşa Mosque (St Catherine's Church)

14thC Lusignan church converted to a mosque. You will be able to see the Lusignan arms with rose and dragon motifs, and decoration of women with fishes on the simpler north entrance.

The Yenicami Mosque

A 14thC church turned into a mosque in 1571, collapsed around 1740, leaving the remains of the minaret and Gothic structures predating that. A new mosque (Yenicami) was built next to the ruins of the old.

The Museum of Barbarism

To find it you need to drive out of town starting at the Venetian Column and turning west past the Colonial Law Courts, through the walls and left on to Osman Pasa. Finally turn north on the Mehmet Akif road and it is on the right, almost opposite the mosque.

This has graphic exhibits detailing an atrocity that occurred during the Cypriot civil war.

On the 24th December 1963, Greek Cypriot irregulars forcibly entered the house of Dr Ilhan, who was a major in the Turkish army, and was on duty that night. The doctor's wife, three children and a neighbour were murdered by machinegun fire, and six neighbours were seriously injured. The house remains almost as it was found that Christmas as a reminder.

This is not for the squeamish or people of a sensitive nature.

10. KARPASIA PENINSULA

The Karpasia Peninsula is also called the '**Pan Handle**' or **Karpazyarimadas**. It has three main names, so that you really feel as if you are going to the end of the world... which you are. It has open spaces, no unfinished husks of buildings, and many wild donkeys. In all the country, this is the remotest and most unspoilt area, and the place you are most likely to see the wildlife.

The Incirli Caves (No. 10 on the map)

Find the village of **Çınarlı** to the north of **Geçitkale.** The caves are natural inside a gypsum hill, and are the largest on the island. There is a hundred metre long passage which contains an amazing collection of stalactites and stalagmites. The cave takes its name from the fig tree nearby, the fruit of which is said to have healing powers. It was reputed to be a hideout for the partisans during the attempts to oust the British.

Iskele (10a)

Iskele (**Trikomo**) is famous for its icon museum. It has a festival in the first two weeks of July and another the first week of August. These are very colourful occasions, and ideal for photo opportunities, but expect extra traffic if you are only passing.

A little further on, the small harbour of **Boğaz** is worth a stop, and fishing boats can be chartered if you want to see the coastline from the water (or go fishing). From here, right along the coast are miles of deserted beaches.

Panagia Kanakaria (10b)

Take a slight detour from the main road up the peninsula to visit the disused church of **Panagia Kanakaria**, (Panagia means 'Blessed Virgin Mary' in Greek and often precedes the name of a church) built on the ruins of a 6th C BC basilica. There were once beautiful mosaics inside, but these disappeared in the late 1970s. It is usually locked up, but the outbuildings are open if sadly devoid of decoration, apart from that left by the occasional bird, but well worth photographs.

If you go further up the road you will come to **Büyükkonuk**, where there is an oil mill dating back to 1870. The mill fell into disuse but was restored in 2008 and reopened as the **Hasder Mill Cultural Centre**. You can see the stages of original olive oil production and also book courses in traditional handicrafts.

Ayios Trias Basilica (10c)

Inland at **Sipahy**, are the ruins of the 5th Century **Ayios Trias Basilica**, which was discovered by accident in 1957, buried on a hilltop. The original building was destroyed by Arab raids in the middle of the 7th Century, and a small church was constructed to the south, using the materials of course. This too was destroyed in the 9-10th Century, and it had remained hidden since then with its mosaic floors virtually intact. These have open access, but try to avoid treading on them; armies of visitors are starting to take their toll.

Unlike the Roman equivalents, the then Christian beliefs insisted on geometric patterns, rather than depictions of daily life (or girls in bikinis — see the **Villa Romana del Casale** in Sicily). There are representations of four-leaf clovers and sandals, and it is surprising how little the design of the latter has changed over nearly two millennia. There is an inscription in one block of mosaic, which is very hard to read, but says that the work was done by Heracleos, one of the deacons.

Dipkarpaz (10d)

The last settlement along the peninsula is one in which Greek Cypriots were allowed to remain after the separation. It is a quiet, unusual place, and has some sad memories of the fighting.

Before 1974, the town was predominantly inhabited by Greek-Cypriots. During the Turkish invasion of Cyprus in 1974, the peninsula was cut off by Turkish troops, and this prevented the town's Greek-Cypriot inhabitants fleeing to the south. As a result, the village had the biggest Greek population in the North. Between 1974 and 1985 however, around 2500 people left the village, but although the Greek-Cypriot population is now mainly elderly and shrinking in size, they are still supplied by the UN, and Greek-Cypriot products are consequently available in some shops. Some properties are now owned by Europeans who favour the wonderfully peaceful lifestyle.

In other parts of the country, there are still some **Greek Cypriot/Mixed villages**. Some Orthodox and some Maronite (Eastern Roman Catholic). The people often stayed because they actually hadn't heard of the fighting, and they have been generally well treated since then. The Turkish Army have a camp enclosing an entire Maronite Village, **Çamlıbel** (Myrtou), near Kyrenia. If you want to visit that and some of the sights, such as **The Blue Villa** (Mavi Kősk), the army will politely ask you to loan them your passport and you will be waved through to visit.

St Andrew's Monastery (10e)

The **Apostolos Andreas Monastery** is at the very end of the peninsula. A new road beyond an unfrequented marina at **Yenierenköy (Parmakli)** stops abruptly and turns into a bumpy farm track. This leads into what is now a wildlife sanctuary for donkeys and their descendants, abandoned when the Greek population was evicted. Try not to run them down as you approach; they will try to stop your vehicle, begging for scraps. If you do share food with them, beware donkey battles as the herd descend; you can get knocked down or cut off by pincer movements once they realise you have things for them to eat (just about everything!)

The legend has it that the ship on which **St Andrew** (then merely an apostle) was travelling to the Holy Land was either desperate for water, lost or shipwrecked, depending on which source you read. Either way, things were looking grim for the sailors. Andrew pointed at the barren shore and said they would find water there. Despite disbelieving cries of "You must be mad," "We're all going

41

to die," and "Pass the Scotch," they landed. Andrew marched forth amidst abuse and mockery, struck a rock with his staff and a spring of water gushed out; they were saved.

"A miracle," they cried as a man, raised him on their shoulders, and built a monastery in his name. History doesn't say if the construction was before or after the Romans crucified him (on an X-shaped cross in **Patras, Greece**) for telling them not to murder people (a common theme in those days), but the building was derelict for many years.

A verifyable incident occurred in 1191. **Berengaria of Navarre** and **Joan Plantagenet**, respectively the fiancée and sister of King Richard 1st, were shipwrecked on Cyprus. **Isaac Komnenos**, the governor, took them captive. In retaliation, Richard conquered the Island while on his way to Lebanon, taking Isaac captive. According to respect, Richard promised Isaac not to put him into irons if he gave himself up without a fight. Isaac duly surrendered and was infuriated to be clapped into chains of silver instead; a little Crusader joke, you might suspect. Richard married Berengaria on May 12, 1191, in the Chapel of St George at **Limassol**. The tables were turned when Richard himself was captured in 1192 by **Duke Leopold V of Austria**, who just happened to be the son of **Theodora Komnene**, (titular?) Queen Consort of Jerusalem and **Isaac's auntie**.

Isaac never did get back to Cyprus, which was now in the hands of the Lusignans, and they wouldn't have returned it, having paid in full. He was poisoned a few years later, presumably for not giving up his claim.

The place of pilgrimage itself is currently (Nov 2015) in three rooms in the outbuildings because the main church has a web of scaffolding round it; you may not be able to get in, or even take a decent photograph. You can light a candle in the makeshift chapel and drop a coin into the box to petition forgiveness.

Despite being there for nearly a millennia, the present building is a relatively new place of multi-faith pilgrimage, after a miracle in 1895. St Andrew appeared to one **Maria Georgiou** in a dream, telling her to go to the monastery to search for her son, kidnapped 17 years earlier. On the crowded boat crossing from Anatolia to Cyprus, she told her tale to a Dervish priest, who showed her his birthmarks revealing that he was actually her missing son; a miracle or coincidence? Whatever the case, the monastery is now visited by pilgrims of many faiths from around the World, and is known as the '**Lourdes of Cyprus**'.

The renovations were not straightforward; there was quite a disagreement when the work began. The **Church of Cyprus** refused to co-operate; a document prepared by the UN failed to name it as the monastery's owner. The Archbishop, **Chrysostomos II** (2006-present), said he would rather see the place fall down than sign up to any plans that didn't make an acknowledgement of their ownership. Finally in 2013 the North Cypriots said they would fund the restoration, and an international team of experts is currently working on it.

11. Güzelyurt

Travel west from Kyrenia along the coast road, eventually taking the most westerly pass through the mountains towards **Çamlibel**.

After the pass, you will see the impressive new **Geçitköy Dam**, a solid sloping arrangement of rocks and concrete on both sides of the barrier. It was virtually empty of water in late 2015, but slowly filling via an undersea pipeline from the Taurus mountains in Turkey, 40 miles away.

The other side of the range is much greener. In the lands beyond the dam there is still some countryside. Even here though, the trees are not tall, mostly a sturdy pine, and widely spaced on the parched and rocky land.

The town of **Güzelyurt** (or **Morfou**, meaning 'Beautiful Land') is in an area famed for its citrus groves. Find the '**Museum of Archaeology and Natural History**'. This has a good collection of stuffed animals, including bizarre mutant lambs, but upstairs is the real prize: a room containing a fabulous hoard of bracelets, rings, necklaces and a gold wreath found in 2005 by the Water Department, constructing a drain behind the **theatre at Soli**. The treasure looks modern, but dates from the Classical and Hellenistic period, 5th to 4th Century BC

Next to the museum is the 18th Century **St Mamas' Church**, which you may need to have unlocked for you to view.

St Mamas

As the story goes, Mamas, a 12th Century holy man, was refusing to pay his taxes. Of course, soldiers duly turned up with a warrant. As they were in the process of hauling him off for an audience with the Duke in Nicosia, he spied a lamb about to become dinner for a lion. Mamas rescued the lamb and leapt on to the lion's back, with the lamb under his arm. Arriving at court, he told the Governor all the reasons why he shouldn't pay tax. Either because of a flawless argument or more likely because he has brought a lion with him, the Governor backed down and granted exemption.

St Mamas thus became the **Patron Saint of Tax Evasion**, and unlike most saints, got off without being martyred, which must be worth something.

There is another Mamas recorded. He also had a lion in a story reminiscent of 'Daniel in the Lion's Den' (and Aesop's Androcles) and was killed around 275 AD in Caesarea (modern day Israel) for his Christian beliefs. His coffin was floated off to sea and recovered when it beached in Cyprus by a local man and his four sons (and two oxen). They dragged it as far as they could, and built a church when the oxen sat down and refused to go any further.

Whatever the real story, his tomb is still in the building, and apparently leaks a substance, which if applied to the ears is said to cure earache and improve the hearing.

Here there is a magnificent display of icons to enjoy.

12. THE PALACE OF VOUNI

Further west still, you have nearly left the country when you see signs for the palace. The road up the outcrop it sits on could be described as 'exciting'. Pray that you don't meet a coach on the way, but once you do get to the top, there is a big carpark and the views are stunning.

Date estimates for the palace vary, but the best evidence points to it being burnt down in 380 BC after an occupation of no more than 120 years. It is believed that the inhabitants were evacuated safely, so this may have been a very early example of 'slighting', especially as the foundations were also partially destroyed.

The information web page, **whatson-northcyprus.com** has a good description of the site, but **cypnet.co.uk** has a much more amusing translation, so is referenced later in preference.

The structure was originally set up around 500 BC by the pro-Persian city state of **Marion** to the west, one of the ten (twelve or thirteen, depending upon source – see 'General Information' later) city kingdoms of Cyprus at the time, as a military base to control the **State of Soli** on the plain below. In 449 BC, the Solians took over the position and it was converted into a palace, eventually consisting of an estimated 137 rooms, including second stories with mud-brick walls, and must have been an impressive sight from the plains below.

"Usually, the ticket boot only sporadically attended" (verbatim from the brochure), so you may get in free.

There are many small walls remaining here, including storerooms with neat sockets for amphorae still visible, and at least three underground cisterns for storing water. Possibly the most remarkable part is the set of steps leading up to what must have been the main entrance. As Cypnet says, and this is verbatim, not spelling mistakes by the author, *"Foctise of the palace is a monumental seven-stepped stairway leading down into a courtyard, where a quitar-sloped stele, slotted at the top for a windlass, is propped on end before a deep eastern."*

It is a lovely setting, perhaps slightly marred by over-large signs telling us where kitchens etc. used to be (really they should have plaques or stones set into the ground). Most of the artefacts were excavated by Swedish archaeologists in the 1920s and can be found in the Stockholm museum.

There is a small covered observation platform on the south side of the carpark. This is normally used for fire watch, a major concern in the area in the hot, dry season. The fires of 1956 and 1995 caused much devastation around Kyrenia, and the newly planted trees are still struggling to catch up with the larger ones in the forest you are now viewing. From here you can see most of the surrounding area:

To the west is an enclave, an area to which the besieged Turkish Cypriots retreated during the troubles, and then the 'Green Line' border, and one of the crossing places.

To the east are the coastal towns, including the short jetty near **Gemikonağı** (meaning 'Anchorage' a good stop for coffee, with its short pier ending in a boat on stilts) and a long one, which allowed copper ore from the now depleted mines at Soli to be loaded directly on to larger ships. At one time the sea was green with copper oxide, and caused the associated devastation of the sea life, but nature has reclaimed her own and now the area looks as clean as any.

To the north lie the Taurus mountains of Turkey 40+ miles away, and to the south the Troodos mountains.

13. SOLI

This site was established early in the 6th Century BC by a Greek called **Solon**, who was a great statesman and law-bringer in Athens, one of his major achievements apparently being the establishment of official brothels. The foundation of the city is described by Plutarch in 75 AD (so is not what you might call a 'primary source') from the translation by John Dryden:

"From thence he (Solon) sailed to Cyprus, where he was made much of by Philocyprus, one of the kings there, who had a small city built by Demophon, Theseus's son, near the river Clarius, in a strong situation, but incommodious and uneasy of access. Solon persuaded him, since there lay a fair plain below, to remove, and build there a pleasanter and more spacious city. And he (Solon) stayed himself, and assisted in gathering inhabitants, and in fitting it both for defence and convenience of living; insomuch that many flocked to Philocyprus, and the other kings imitated the design; and, therefore, to honour Solon, he called the city Soli, which was formerly named Aepea."

Soli is traditionally the place where **St Mark was baptised**, possibly in the very basilica you visit. This is covered by a huge roof to protect the magnificent mosaics from the elements. Raised walkways have been installed to keep your boots from damaging them. As with the previous basilica, the patterns are mostly geometric, but here have been added swans, dolphins and a strange type of duck which causes much discussion as to its breed.

The basilica itself was built in the 4th Century AD on an earlier structure. It was then destroyed in the 5th and rebuilt, then dedicated to **St Auxibios**, who was Soli's first appointed bishop (57 AD). The city was finally abandoned after being destroyed during Arab raids of 647 and 649 AD. As usual, the masonry from the ruined city was plundered and used for other buildings. Between 1859-68, stones from the site were shipped over to Egypt and used in the reconstruction of **Port Said**.

Above the basilica is a reconstructed **Greco-Roman theatre**. The stage is in a condition which you could use for producing Othello, although the absence of changing rooms would make it interesting. The theatre is still used for occasional performances, which must be quite a spectacle with the views beyond. There is a strange plank-covered channel in the middle, front to back, and no real explanation is offered for this.

There are other excavations at Soli, which have uncovered a temple to Athena, the market place, and a necropolis from whence came the amazing golden headdress in the Güzelyurt museum, but there are also concerns about vandalism and plunder, so most of the rest of the site is still inaccessible, though still worth a detailed visit.

14. KANTARA CASTLE

Although Kantara is the easternmost castle, part of the Karpaz, it deserves a separate visit.

Take the coast road along to **Kaplica**, and then turn right up what looks like a road to a farm; don't be discouraged by the signage; even the travel brochures say to ignore the signs and follow your instinct. The newly-made road up the side of the mountain is breaking up slightly, but at least it's double width to the village of **Kantara**.

The village is largely deserted. The British built it for forest wardens and castle custodians, and there are a number of pleasant and empty properties available, should you wish to live half a kilometre up a mountain and 8Km from the nearest shop. There is however a smart restaurant, recommended for lunch.

The rest of the road is single-track through a sparse forest up to the castle itself.

The easternmost of the Byzantine watchtowers, Kantara Castle, commands both sides of the Karpaz Peninsula. The first official records are from 1191 when **Isaac Comnenos** holed up, and subsequently, as well as being the lookout, it was frequently a refuge for defeated overlords. It continued in use when the Venetians took over, but was in disrepair by 1562, as the fortifications of Kyrenia, Famagusta and Nicosia became the main defences against the artillery then in use.

The last major improvements were made by **James I of Cyprus** between 1382 and 1398 and these are the parts that you can still see.

It is the lowest of the three Crusader castles, but as good as any. At the highest point, the watchtower at 630m, you have 360 degree views across the country. On a clear winter day, it is said you can see snow on the mountains of Lebanon. Of old, from here, flares and fires would alert the capital that raiders were approaching. You can normally see the coastline to Kyrenia, the bay of Famagusta and the Karpaz peninsula, as well as Nicosia in the far distance and the Troodos and Taurus Mountains. There is supposed to be a ghost, a queen sitting in the window of the watchtower, but there are no more details to be found as to who she might be.

Many rooms are still mostly intact, and there are cisterns which still collect water a thousand years after they were built. Kantara was definitely a military outpost. One feels nothing other than martial presence here; barracks and defences only.

The most impressive part is the horseshoe bastion, which has two comfortable antechambers leading to a narrow room with seven arrow slits, covering every angle of approach. You could hold off an entire army from here, as long as they left their cannons behind.

The military toilets are still visible; a hole in the wall emptying down the cliff. None of your Roman luxury here, with running water. Resist the temptation to try them out; there are better ones at the ticket office.

15. BUFFAVENTO

If you have time, and fancy another climb, visit Buffavento Castle, which is the highest of the three Crusader castles at nearly 1000m. This was again originally a Byzantine watchtower turned into a castle in the 12th Century. The Lusignans used it mainly as a prison, enticingly entitled the '**Chateau du Lion**'.

Of the three, Buffavento is in the worst state of repair owing to its altitude and the constant buffeting of the winds, from which it gets its name. There is graffiti, not present at the others. In times of old it can't have been much fun here. One story recounts a **John Visconti** in the mid-1360s. The then queen, **Eleanor of Aragon**, (1333-1416) was supposed to be having a fling with a noble called **John de Morf**. Visconti told the king, **Peter 1st** (1328-1369), and rather than thanking him kindly and buying him a drink, Peter had Visconti flung (eventually) into Buffavento dungeons to starve to death. Visconti would have been pleased to know that Peter himself was murdered by nobles, possibly led by John de Morf (and Eleanor) worried about the same thing happening to them. Peter was a quite good 'flinger' we hear.

The castle fell into disuse when the Venetians took over, as with the other two, and quickly became a ruin. It narrowly missed destruction in devastating forest fires of 1995.

Check before you try to visit, as the Army control entry days, and you know how good they are with their guns! Also beware the road, which is not in the best state of repair.

16. EAST OF KYRENIA

Tatlisu Byzantine Church (16a)

For a separate trip, take the coast road east, and stop at another Byzantine church near the village of Tatlisu (Freshwater). This has virtually intact murals, but in the gardens you will find the most delightful models of many of the major attractions you can see on your travels. See if you can identify strange flowers like red velvet pompoms and let the author know; nobody else seems to.

There is more archaeology is going on outside the fence; it looks like the site was originally quite extensive. Evidence of out-buildings is still being unearthed. It would have been a private monastery complex in Byzantine days.

This museum has only just been opened (July 2015) and currently there are no English reviews.

Antiphonitis Church at Esentepe (16b)

Five kilometres south-east of Esentepe village up a very windy road is the 7th Century Antiphonitis Church. This still has a few of its lovely frescoes to view, although sadly damaged by (Greek) graffiti.

It used to be the centre of an influential monastery. Because of its unusual design, it is thought to have been built by local artists.

The narthex (enclosed entrance passage) to the west and gallery to the south were added by the Lusignans in the 14th or 15thC.

The dome is on eight round columns which form an irregular octagon. The altar area was separated from the rest of the church with two of the columns away from the walls.

The building is one of the finest of its kind in Cyprus. The cloister arrangement in the south is a unique example of Gothic stonework.

The Armenian Monastery (16c)

The Armenian monastery of **Sourp Magar** was first established in about 1000 AD as a **Coptic** (Egyptian Christian) monastery, and was dedicated to the Egyptian hermit **St Makarios of Alexandria** (309-404 AD) whose monastery still exists in Egypt.

It is about 100m away from the **Kyrenia Herbarium**, up the road from **Karaağaç**. You can also get there from the main Arapkoy road, but this may be a bit of a climb.

It was also used as a summer resort by the Armenian Church in the early 15th Century and became a favourite pilgrimage spot for Armenians on their way to and from the Holy Land until 1974.

Outside a wall on the eastern side is a pillar with an inscription in the Armenian language dated 1933.

It has a picnic area outside, but take your lunch into the buildings themselves and enjoy the peace there. Please do take your litter home though – there are few rubbish collections, and the bags will blow out to sea and choke turtles.

17. ESSENTIAL SUPPLIES

These deserve a section of their own. Apart from the things you usually take, such as toothbrush, soap and a Lego pirate ship, you will need the following:

- Insect repellent – people's bodies vary, so try a few out until you get one that suits you, and works of course.
- Antihistamine tablets and cream and a healing gel such as Aloe Vera from Boots.
- Baby wipes or wet wipes for mopping blood and dirt
- First aid kit, containing plasters, antiseptic cream, scissors, brandy and anything else that comes with it.
- Imodium or other stopper of the 'squits'. (Don't take too much or you will end up the other way, with the 'clenches'.)
- Mosquito zapper - Plug-in or otherwise for your room to stop being bitten while asleep
- 'No More Nails' to repair the fittings in your two-star hotel.
- SIM card for your phone, to lock on to the local signals.
- Water in bottles. In a warm country essential. One of the early signs of dehydration is a headache, so drink lots and keep off the paracetamol. You will also need bottled water to clean teeth and add to your Scotch.
- A travel kettle for boiling the water and making a nice cup of tea.
- Powdered coffee and milk – local milk is usually 'long life'.
- A small LED torch for exploring caves and tombs.

18. GENERAL INFORMATION

Amphorae

And why are they pointy at the bottom? Looking at the elliptic cross-section of the ship in **Kyrenia Castle**, you can see that there was no flat deck and with the curvature of the hull, the amphorae rested on their sides. They could therefore pack more in, owing to the bottom of the boat being narrower than the top. This means that most transportation of goods was by sea in those days. Another benefit of having no deck is that the centre of gravity is lower when loaded. This keeps the ship more stable and removes the need for the extra ballast used in later flat deck ships.

Atatürk

Mustafa Kemal Atatürk (1881-1938) founded the Independent Republic of Turkey after the Ottoman Empire was dissolved, fighting on the side of Germany in **World War 1**. Struggling for independence against Greek occupiers, and using Russian supplies, Mustafa succeeded in beating them and the Armenians, and forced the Allies occupying Istanbul to sign a favourable peace treaty. He then served as Turkey's first president from 1923, implementing reforms that westernized the nation, and shrinking the role of Islam in public. But although the country was moving towards democracy, he could sometimes be a dictator. He was given the honorary title, **Atatürk**, meaning 'Father of the Turks' in 1934 and died 10th November 1938.

Beaches

The North has a number of excellent beaches. Despite the hype (http://www.cyprusholidayadvisor.com/beaches.htm), beware; those in popular places do not seem to be maintained, with litter a major problem, even though they have facilities for washing and showering after a dip. Most of the information on the Net seems to be focused on the South. The Mediterranean in general is used as a rubbish dumping ground by most of the surrounding countries, and they obviously like to share their litter.

There are other reported hazards such as Jellyfish, Sea Urchins and Weaver fish, but these are very rare. Even so, if swimming, it is a good idea to wear foot protection.

Beer

This is of course not ale, but a pilsner. The only one available seems to be the Turkish **EFES**, which fortunately is strong and goes well with Cypriot food and weather.

It comes in several varieties, but the Pils seems to be the most popular drink. Most places will serve it, but some die-hard establishments boycott, whereupon the best alternative is the local wine and water.

Another type of EFES called Fıcı, which is the draft beer and not so fizzy, and usually comes in generous measures, especially if accompanied by food.

From the bottle beer comes at 500ml (or 330 if you choose something out of the ordinary), but if on draught, you get a better deal as there are no apparent measurement restrictions, and you can end up with as much as 750ml to quench your thirst. Expect to pay half what it would cost in the UK for this, so it goes down all the better for it.

At current rates (2015/6) you can pay from 6-8 Lira for a half litre.

Border Crossings

There are six on the map, and currently free access is allowed 24 hours a day, although expect night crossings to be treated with suspicion and bleary gazes. West to east:

Limnitis (Yeşilırmak) the most western crossing on the coast beyond Soli.

Astromeritis/Bostanci/Zodhia (car only) – south of **Morphou-Güzelyurt.**

Metehan (also called Agios Dometios or Kermiya) in the west of Nicosia: A crossing point for vehicle, bicycle or foot.

Ledra Street (or Palace) (Central Nicosia, pedestrians only) - opened on 3 April 2008 and now the most central of all crossings.

Pergamos/Beyarmudu/Dhekylia in the British Eastern Sovereign Base area, south of **Agdogan**.

Strovilia or Akyar near **Agios Nikolaos** - also in a Base at the eastern part of the island near Famagusta.

Brandy

The local brandy is to be recommended, so do try it. It is not as strong as French Brandy, being little over 30% on average, and is produced by double distillation of white wine and aging in oak barrels.

Brandy Sour

The cocktail was original produced at the Forest Park Hotel, in Plátres on the southern slopes of the Troodos, for King Farouk of Egypt. He used it to hide his enjoyment of alcohol from his Muslim subjects; it is made to look like tea.

Ingredients:
50 ml Cyprus brandy
25 ml undiluted lemon cordial
25 ml lemonade
2-3 dashes Angostura® bitters
soda water

Pour the Brandy into a long glass
Add the undiluted cordial and mix well
Add 2 dashes of Angostura bitters to each glass
Mix well again before adding ice
Top up with soda water
Add slice of lemon, and stir

Drink, enjoy and pretend it's tea if any Methodists spot you.

The British

The attitude to the Brits varies. Recently the Turkish Cypriots were actually talking of wanting the British back – there are still some British bases in South Cyprus. They felt that having a neutral force present would help with relations both with the South and Turkey. There is still some animosity between Greek and Turkish Cypriots, but this is passive now thank the Lord/Allah etc. If you ask the more militant Greeks, they will tell you that the North is the source of all their problems, oh, and the US and Turkey, who are entirely to blame for everything else, and not the British.

Cabin Baggage

Why do people on the plane need whopping great wheeled bags, which surely must contain the Crown Jewels, kitchen sinks, cannonballs and induction motors for electric buses, judging by the struggle they have to get them into the overhead lockers? Boarding would be so much quicker if they left them in the hold and just sat down, instead of dithering about in the aisles. Take a spear with you for prodding selfish people out of the way, and make sure that you only carry essentials on the plane.

Cakes, Sweetmeats and Diets

In all of North Cyprus (and Turkey), cakes are something special. There are many different types; they are all delicious and beg to be tried. Expect to weigh a bit more when you return from your holiday.

Camera Batteries

There are always lots of things to take pictures of, but do check your camera. What power cells does it take? If you have something not available in any shops, take a charger with you and put the camera on charge *every* night. The best solution though is to have a camera that takes normal AA batteries. Spares can then be picked up cheaply at general goods stores.

Central Plains of Cyprus

Vast and arid, with settlements scattered about in unlikely places. This used to be a forested area, but man has cut the lot down. There are odd rows of eucalyptus trees planted to shade and drain the narrow-gauge railway built by the British in the 19[th]C for ferrying goods from the main port at Famagusta to the interior. This has long since been removed.

Once the rains come, the growing season starts and the plain turns to lush green, with many wild flowers owing to the pleasing lack of intensive farming. Spring is a wonderful time to visit.

City Kingdoms in Cyprus

There are conflicting reports here. Traditionally there were ten kingdoms, but some sources list twelve, say ten and give thirteen names.

It is likely that Kyrenia was its own kingdom for a while, but here is the approximate layout of twelve of them in 500 BC, boiled down from various sources.

Exchange rates

Turkish Lire currently (Nov 2015) about 4 to the UK Pound, but you can get a better rate from banks and ATMs in the North Cyprus local high street. Selling them back to the bank, again you will get a better rate before you leave.

Flags

Note that the North Cyprus flag looks like the Turkish but the colour are inverted.

Flights

A lot of the British travel companies bring people in via the South but Turkish airlines such as Cyprus Paradise and Green Island will bring you to **Ercan Airport** to the east of Nicosia. They advertise a

'Direct' flight from **Stansted** (Pegasus) and **Luton** (AtlasJet), but there is an intermediate landing at Istanbul's second airport, **Sabiha Gökçen**. You will sit on the plane whilst they change flight numbers and crews and to all intent it now emulates an internal flight. Allow extra time, but if you like flying, it is more fun!

Footwear, Clothing and Sun-block

Walking boots and cotton trousers are recommended. The boots because many surfaces are uneven; even those you think are fine tend to have hidden traps. The trousers because there are small sand-flies that will give you a nip and can make your leg swell up.

For the same reason take a hat with a large brim. Not only does this keep the sun off your head, but the flies can only approach from limited directions.

Finally, apply a decent amount of sun-block to exposed flesh. Even in winter, the radiation can be strong.

The Guide

This book will be your guide. While not as much use as a local who knows where you are going, you can still stop and ask if you get lost, pointing at the section in the book if the locals don't speak English (most of them do). Failing that, look for the familiar landmarks of Five Finger Mountain or any of the three castles, visible from most places in the North.

Heathrow

Landing: Allow a minimum of 90 minutes after the flight lands before trying to get a mainline train from most London terminals.

Recommendations: **Book a room** in a hotel at Heathrow and stay overnight, starting again in the morning when chirpy staff are happy to help... or

Park your own transport in one of the extortionately priced local facilities and return to that for your escape... or

Get a kind friend or family member to rescue you... or

Fly from somewhere else!

Taking off is easier. Simply make sure you are there in plenty of time. Terminal 5 is fast and efficient.

Hire Cars

You will need a current UK or international driving license to get one, and there are centres in all the main towns. Search terms **"North Cyprus Rent a Car"** for a list.

These are a great way to see the country, especially if you are from the UK, because sensibly they still drive on the left. However, note that there will be lots of other tourist drivers about, and they might be from other countries and aren't as level-headed as you.

Watch out for **cars with red number plates**, because these are hire cars, like the one you are driving.

Watch out for **trucks**, because they are driven by mad kamikaze pilots – your red number plate is like a target for them.

Watch out for **potholes**. Roads are a little lumpy in places, so you can't drive fast, and locations take a lot longer to get to than you would think. The country is, after all, only 100 Km (60 miles) long, about the same length and surface area as Cornwall, but without the direct roads, and you know what Cornish miles are like (they seem to go on forever).

Watch out for **speed cameras**. There aren't many of these and they are always preceded by warning signs. Don't ignore them.

If you do crash, you have to wait with the wreckage until the police come, but the locals will stop and ask if you need help, so don't feel too worried.

Health and Safety

In Cyprus they are sensible. There might be a sign telling you, English language included, not to be a complete dingbat and fall off a wall, but there won't be serious barriers, barbed wire and machine-gun posts preventing you. Take care; your life is in your own hands.

The Internet

Some hotels provide free Wi-Fi, which you can connect to. This may not be as fast as you are used to in the UK, so you will need to be patient.

The Language

It is only polite to learn a bit of the local language. Here are a few useful words - with English pronunciation in brackets:

Giriş	- Way in ('girish')
Çıkış	- Way out (cickush)
Merhaba	- Hello (mare-haba) or use the English 'Hello'
Günaydın	- Good morning (g-niden)
İyi geceler	- Good night (e-gege-lair)
Hoşça kal	- Goodbye (horch-cha-kal) or use Bye-bye
Lütfen	- Please (lootfan)
Teşekkür ederim	- Thank you (te-sheh-cour e-derim)
Yok	- No (E-ock)
Özür dilerim	- I'm sorry (U-zur day-lerim)
Ben bir içki içebilirler Lütfen	- Please can I have a drink (ban berichti ichey-birelar lute-fan)
Yüksük	- Thimble (Yooksook)
Eğer bir yüksük var?	- Have you a thimble? (Ayar bir yuksic vash)
Park yapılmaz	- No parking (park upilmus)
Hız kamerası	- Speed camera (huth camirus-th)
Sınır kontrolü	- Border control (sunih control-yuh)

It is perhaps not advisable to try all these out on border guards or policemen until you have been on a real language course, but you will make the shopkeepers smile at least.

Mobiles

Your mobile is unlikely to work unless you buy a SIM for the local providers. Even then, you may have trouble getting a signal. Probably better to use hotel Wi-Fi on your fondleslab if you are that keen on keeping in touch with the rest of the world. Don't forget though that a holiday is supposed to be a break from normal life to allow you to unwind.

Money and Prices

North Cyprus uses the Turkish Lira, which is legal tender only there and in Turkey. You can buy a lot of stuff with it, most things being on average 30% cheaper than the UK, especially petrol, which looks a bargain compared to our own; something to bear in mind if you want to hire a car.

Most shops will also accept Euros and Sterling, although the exchange rates might not be as good as you would hope. Watch out for items priced in Euros and not Lira. The recommendation is to always use Lira to pay with as there are usually no misunderstandings.

The moment you cross the border into South Cyprus, your Lira are not accepted; Sterling is, but by the time you get to the airport, the Euro seems to be the preferred currency. Either spend or change your Lira before you cross the border, or keep the notes to exchange back home at less favourable rates.

Mosquitos, gnats and other nibblers

For the night get a plug-in electric zapper. This uses ultraviolet light to attract the little abominations and then electrocute them. Cruel perhaps, but they don't think of the upset they cause when they abandon their usual prey of plants and shrubs and pick on us mammals.

For the day, use insect repellent, a quick reaction and a big hat. If you get bitten, try Aloe Vera Gel from Boots to sooth the pain, and antihistamine tablets and cream.

At **Salamis** we were probably nibbled by **sand-flies**. These little horrors can sometimes carry **sand-fly fever**, which in severe cases can land you in hospital. Note that the last reports of it in Cyprus were from 2002, so don't panic or be put off. You never see or hear a sand-fly but they have a bite like a one star review for your travel-guide on Amazon and can leave a large bump and a bit of a hole if you are susceptible. Fortunately most people aren't. The females have the larger jaws and carry the infection, which can take 3 weeks to get out of your system, and has flu-like symptoms. **Sand-fly fever** is to be found in many eastern Mediterranean countries, so it is well to be aware and take precautions wherever you go.

No More Nails

Take a small tube of this with you. In North Cyprus, the standard of maintenance men rises occasionally to the level of 'It'll Do'. Just about all the fittings and fixtures are loose, or missing the odd screw. There is nothing dangerous, but a quick application of a fixing agent will make it so much better. Feel free to do this and generally tidy up during your stay.

The Nose and Head

Pressure differences when flying can be painful, more so if you have sinus problems, or a slight cold. Take one of those little bottles of decongestant, and have a good sniff before take-off and others during the flight if required. Decongestant tablets are not as effective under these conditions and can make you feel groggy.

Origins of the name, Cyprus

The most likely is that it was named after the copper mines which have been in operation since the Bronze Age and only closed in the 1970s. Of course, the converse is that the metal might have been named after the island, **Kupros**, and where **Aphrodite** (also called **Kypris**) fits in is anybody's guess. One might suspect though that copper was found elsewhere in the world, so probably the first explanation is the one to go for.

There are new moves to resume mining, although with anti-pollution rules, sea life will be less at risk than it was back then. There is still one long ship-loading pier to be seen on the north coast near **Gemikonaği**.

Pigging out

The food is excellent, plentiful and cheap, but watch out for the puddings; these are tasty but normally very sweet and you might suspect, quite fattening. You may find yourself eating three big meals a day, and for anyone outside of teenage years, this is not a good idea. Try to moderate your intake and not have to buy two seats for the return journey.

Place Names

Because of the history, towns in the North tend to have both a Greek and Turkish name. This was a mixed community until 1974. They are in many cases used interchangeably. Famagusta is 'Gazimağusa' in Turkish (pronounced rather like 'Gazimauser' as the ğ in Turkish is silent) and Kyrenia is Girne. The locals use both when chatting. Other examples are Alsançak (Turkish) being Karavas (Greek). Bellapais is Belerbeyi.

Power sockets

These are the same as in the UK, as a result of the British apparently having invented electricity. Lots of things seem familiar, from the traffic lights, to driving on the left and the traffic jams, which is one of the attractions; the country has a 1950s feel to it.

Religion

North Cyprus is a Muslim country. Despite the fact that all the big Lusignan churches have been converted to mosques and all the Byzantine chapels have been locked up, nobody seems to take any notice. Yes, in mosques you have to dispense with your shoes (so make sure your socks are darned), the women have to cover their heads, and everyone has to have their knees removed, but nobody really seems to bother if these conventions (apart from the shoes) are not observed.

Seasons and Weather

Summer is mighty hot, with temperatures going over 40C. If you go then, you may find yourself spending all your time beside the pool or in and out of the sea. If you don't mind this, then North Cyprus is as hot as anywhere around the Mediterranean, and a lot cheaper.

Spring and Autumn are the best times to visit for sightseeing (May or early November), as the attractions are usually all open, and the weather is more pleasant.

Later in the year, expect brisk breezes and rainstorms, but you will find the sun hot. This gives you the problem of needing to wear a hat, but also having to hang on to it to prevent it blowing away. You need a light coat or jumper to keep out the breeze, but also a bag to put it in when you find shelter, or the wind changes. Temperatures in early November can go up to 30 Centigrade but the nights are chilly through the winter. Expect the rains to come about mid-month.

Winter is probably best for trekking. Take a woolly, it can get very cold at night, decent rainwear and walking boots for protection against the elements up in the mountains.

Stray animals

There are plenty of cats and dogs wandering loose. The oxymoronic concept of a 'registered stray' is a tag on a dog's ear provided by the charity, **Kyrenia Animal Rescue**, who are carrying out a campaign for neutering. This has its animal centre under the **Beşparmak** (Five Finger Mountain) and is run by British Ex-pats. It also takes cats, neutering and marking the ears so that they are not recaptured after freeing them back into their original locations.

There is no report of rabies on the island, but it is advisable not to make too much of a fuss of the animals, although you can adopt them if you wish, subject to all the normal regulations in your home country.

Tea and coffee

Most foreign hotels of lower star rating do not have tea-making facilities. It is worth buying a simple travel kettle and taking your own tea, coffee and favourite creamer. These are quite light so they improve your luggage weight by taking up the space you might feel inclined to use for storing gold bars, cannon balls and diving boots. It is well worth it for a nice cup of tea.

If you want **decaffeinated**, take your own. The very mention in a café can result in horror and outrage, unless it is a very good one, when your wallet might feel a little lighter after the bill (but then we don't go to that kind of establishment, do we?).

Practise using the kettle before you go, and try out a number of whiteners until you find the one that works best. Use bottled water in the tests to mimic battle conditions.

Make sure you have the right power adapter for your kettle if visiting other countries. Cyprus of course sensibly uses the standard UK 3-pin plug.

Note that if you take your teabags to cafés, you can ask for hot water, but it is best to buy lots of other things there to compensate for the embarrassment.

The local tea is **Chai**, which is an acquired taste, and may taste different from that you can get in the UK.

Turkish coffee should be supplied with a glass of water to drink with it – an old tradition.

Television

Take a good book. Turkish TV is somewhat limited in its subject matter. If you are lucky and the TV in your room works, and receives a signal, you can connect to the **BBC World Service** for news, and weather across the Indian sub-continent (they don't seem to cover Turkey), or to one channel which broadcasts wholesome American shows with Turkish subtitles.

As a better alternative, I would recommend you leave you room and go down to the harbour to sip EFES and 'people watch'. You will soon make lots of friends in the form of the guys who are there to persuade you to sit in their own particular café. Some of them are keen to learn English, so remember those magic phrases to share with them (know what I mean, John).

Time Factors

Cyprus is **two hours ahead of the UK**. This means you can stay up later without feeling tired. It also means you have to get up very early in the morning if you want to travel any distance and arrive before your destination closes or night falls.

Traffic Lights and Speed Cameras

The lights seem to be respected by most of the traffic, as are the speed cameras. Be aware though that if those in an area are switched off, this could be because the central electricity producer has cut the power because the police have not paid their bill. In this case, you are unlikely to be hounded for speeding. However, because the speed cameras are usually placed as safety features, rather than in the UK, mostly to milk cash out of otherwise law-abiding citizens, it is wise to slow down and at least be aware of the hazards they protect.

Transport

If you haven't hired a car, you can use **Taxis**, which are friendly, most of the drivers speak English and quite cheap, especially if you share the fare with your chums or negotiate a week's travel in advance, or you can use the **Dolmuş**. These are minibuses that wander all over the area without a fixed timetable, and you can travel for a few Lira. They leave from behind the main carpark in

Kyrenia, but you can hail one at any point on its route and it will stop for you. When you want to get off, you shout and they obligingly hold up all the traffic behind as you pay them a few coppers and climb out. The destination is usually in large writing somewhere on the outside, so if you want excitement and mystery, leap on the first one that appears and see where it takes you. The state of the vehicles varies from total decrepitude to streamlined elegance but they are great fun to travel on.

Make sure you have plenty of change in your pocket – a journey approximately costs 3-4 Lira, but you may pay a bit more if you need to 'bribe' the driver to take you further... to Karpaz for example (and bring you back).

Tourist Offices

In many places in the World, these are an essential visit. There are nearly always armfuls of literature to help you around the country. Invariably the custodians speak English and are only too happy to help you find your way.

Tourist Office Locations

Kyrenia by the old harbour in Kyrenia, tel: +90 392 8152145
Famagusta by the Land Gate (the main entrance to Famagusta old town), tel: +90 392 366 2864
Ercan Airport: +90 392 231 4737
Nicosia inside the Kyrenia Gate.
London Northern Cyprus Tourist Office: 0207-631-1930

Turtles

Several of the beaches in the north are protected breeding grounds for turtles. The Green Turtle (Chelonia mydas) and the Loggerhead Turtle (Caretta Caretta) are both endangered species, and there are protection patrols at breeding times when the hatchlings make the perilous dash to the sea. Cyprus was probably the first country in the Mediterranean to legally protect turtles, along with dolphins and seals, by passing legislation in 1971. You can volunteer to help the **Society for the Protection of Turtles**: http://cyprusturtles.org/volunteering.php if you submit an application in advance.

Turkish Delight

Comes in many flavours and not just 'rose' or 'lemon' like we get in the UK. There is a comprehensive shop in the covered market (**Bandabulya**) in Nicosia, but many others will have a selection.

Water

Although it is treated for the taps, it is best to stick with bottled water. Most hotels have storage tanks on the roof, and the water is only as clean as the tank, bearing in mind these are in direct sunlight all day. Expect your hotel to charge up to four times the amount from the local shop. Despite that, drink plenty. It is still cheaper than in the UK, which is surprising really, considering the amount of the stuff that comes out of our skies for free. Remember that one of the earliest signs of dehydration to recognise is a headache, so be on your guard.

Wildlife

The main winged creatures seem to be **Hooded Crows**, but you may see other familiar birds if you look. A garden with pond and/or fountain will attract them. For wilder creatures, **Karpaz** is the best place the year round, with donkeys, horses and birds to see. Cyprus is on several migration routes, so at the right time of the year, you will see more unusual birds. There is also a wide variety of plants to identify.

Wild Sheep

The Mouflon was introduced to Cyprus during the Neolithic period and was (and probably still is) hunted for 'sport'. It acquired a mystical status for a while, but now there are thought to be less than 3000 animals still in the wild, mostly in Karpaz.

Wine

As with most places, if you talk nicely to the café owners, they may share some of their home brew with you. This varies from good to excellent, and sometimes they can be persuaded to sell you a carafe to take away. Don't expect to get it home; you will have drunk it and/or shared with your fellow explorers long before that happens. Even so, you have a nice glass souvenir to remind you to come back again someday. It is said that people never visit North Cyprus only once.

19. REFERENCES

Aiya Sophia: http://www.cyprus44.com/nicosia/sophia-cathedral.asp

Annan Peace Plan:
http://www.rferl.org/content/article/1102471.html

Antiphonitis Church: http://www.whatson-northcyprus.com/interest/kyrenia/antiphonitis.htm

Ataturk: http://www.history.com/topics/kemal-ataturk

St Andrew's Monastery (and tat stalls):
http://www.360cities.net/image/apostolos-andreas-monastery-karpaz-cyprus

Ataturk: http://www.allaboutturkey.com/ataturk.htm

Saint Barnabas: http://www.whatson-northcyprus.com/interest/famagusta/salamis/barnabas.htm

Beaches: http://www.cyprusholidayadvisor.com/beaches.htm

Beach Safety:
http://cyprus.angloinfo.com/information/lifestyle/sports-and-leisure/beach-sea-safety/

Bellapais Abbey: http://www.sacred-destinations.com/cyprus/bellapais-abbey

Birds of Cyprus: http://www.birdlifecyprus.org/

Blue Villa: http://cyprusscene.com/2012/11/26/camlibels-hidden-gem-the-mavi-kosk-the-blue-villa/

Border Crossings: http://www.cyprus-travel-secrets.com/cyprus-border-crossings.html

Brandy Sour: http://www.cypruskeysadvisers.net/brandy-sour.html

Buffavento Castle:
http://www.cyprus44.com/kyrenia/buffavento-castle.asp

Caterina Cornaro:
https://en.wikipedia.org/wiki/Catherine_Cornaro
Cyprus - general information:
http://www.worldatlas.com/webimage/countrys/europe/cy.htm
Cyprus Timeline:
http://www.cypnet.co.uk/ncyprus/history/index.html
Ghost Town - Famagusta:
http://www.telegraph.co.uk/news/worldnews/europe/cyprus/11
038580/Famagusta-the-ghost-town-at-the-heart-of-Cyprus.html
St Hilarion Castle:
http://www.cypnet.co.uk/ncyprus/city/kyrenia/castle/sthilarion/
History of Cyprus:
http://www.heureka.clara.net/cyprus/history.htm
Islam - Reformation of: http://nypost.com/2015/03/22/activist-
argues-for-a-complete-reformation-of-islam/
Kantara Castle: http://www.cyprus44.com/famagusta/kantara-
castle.asp
Kyrenia Animal Rescue http://www.kartrnc.org/
Lusignans: http://www.cypnet.co.uk/ncyprus/history/lusignan/
St Mamas: http://www.whatson-
northcyprus.com/interest/guzelyurt/mamas.htm
Map of Cyprus:
https://en.wikipedia.org/wiki/File:Cyprus_topo.png
Mevlana Celaleddin-i Rumi: http://mevlana.net/index.html
Music Festival, Bellapais. http://www.bellapaisfestival.com/
Nicosia: https://en.wikipedia.org/wiki/Nicosia
North Cyprus Tourism: www.welcometonorthcyprus.org
Othello Tower and Castle:
http://www.cyprus44.com/famagusta/othello-tower.asp
Ottoman Sultans:
https://en.wikipedia.org/wiki/List_of_sultans_of_the_Ottoman_E
mpire
Salamis: http://romeartlover.tripod.com/Salamis.html

Solon: http://classics.mit.edu/Plutarch/solon.html
Sufism: http://www.nimatullahi.org/what-is-sufism/
Tahini: http://www.cyprus-travel-secrets.com/cyprus-dips.html
Third Crusade: http://www.lordsandladies.org/the-third-crusade.htm
Turkish Stars: http://www.sky-flash.com/stars/index.html
Turtles: http://cyprusturtles.org/
Vouni Palace: http://travelerati.com/vouni-palace-cyprus/
Water Supply Project:
https://en.wikipedia.org/wiki/Northern_Cyprus_Water_Supply_Project
Whirling Dervishes: http://whatson-northcyprus.com/interest/nicosia/north_nicosia/mevlevi_tekke.htm
Yirmisekiz Celebi Tomb: http://www.whatson-northcyprus.com/interest/famagusta/famagusta/yirmisekiz.htm

See also: http://wikitravel.org/en/Northern_Cyprus

ABOUT THE AUTHOR

Robert Wingfield is a wordsmith who likes to turn his hand to many different genres. He has produced children's books and short stories, Gothic and chillers, and a series of satirical science fiction works, as well as factual pieces, travel guides and book reviews. All have the underlying humour that characterises his writing. To date (2016) he has 14 works available via Amazon.

In order to help other authors get their works into print, he founded the Inca Project, which is a free resource for struggling authors, he and the other main members contribute to, when not writing their own books.

www.incaproject.co.uk

He is also a proof reader and copy editor and provides regular input to the Chartered Management Institute

This book is part of the One Man in a Pocket series, which are intended to be pocket guides around the main sights in various countries.

www.cantbearsd.co.uk

7476906R00053

Printed in German
by Amazon Distribu
GmbH, Leipzig